SOULFUL
100 Poems
on Love, Faith, and Life

About the Author

Rhodesia has written poetry since the tender age of three, was once hailed as Philippines' Youngest Author at the age of nine, having compiled an anthology of poems. Her writing craft paused when she focused on clinical, academic, and administrative duties as a physician. Currently a devoted mother of two, she has rejuvenated her love for the written word.

Rhodesia

SOULFUL
100 Poems
on Love, Faith, and Life

Vanguard Press

VANGUARD PAPERBACK

© Copyright 2024
Rhodesia

The right of Rhodesia to be identified as author of this work has been asserted by her in accordance with the Copyright, Designs and Patents Act 1988.

All Rights Reserved

No reproduction, copy or transmission of this publication may be made without written permission.
No paragraph of this publication may be reproduced, copied or transmitted save with the written permission of the publisher, or in accordance with the provisions of the Copyright Act 1956 (as amended).

Any person who commits any unauthorised act in relation to this publication may be liable to criminal prosecution and civil claims for damages.

A CIP catalogue record for this title is available from the British Library.

ISBN 978 1 80016 901 2

*Vanguard Press is an imprint of
Pegasus Elliot Mackenzie Publishers Ltd.*
www.pegasuspublishers.com

First Published in 2024

**Vanguard Press
Sheraton House Castle Park
Cambridge England**

Printed & Bound in Great Britain

PREFACE

Poetry is a language of the soul. In the kaleidoscope of human emotions and expressions, I choose to share my hue and point of view in this language, hoping that this book may add to the richness and beauty of the human experience. If I may touch a heart or stir a soul in the process, I consider my life well-lived.

There is no specific arrangement, whether logical or temporal, of the poems. The reader is invited to experience this book like standing before the ocean, with the poems as waves in succession. Some of these poems were written a long time ago; others only recently. However, I am not an avid believer of the linearity of time as to past, present, or future, much as I don't patronize surnames which may define or change. I consider it a kindness and a courtesy that I may be recognized by my first name only.

Finally, let me dedicate this book to you, my dear reader, to my mother, my children, my one true love, and all those who also believe in the purity and power of love and faith.

Contents

OUR LOVE	13
I WILL LOVE YOU	14
ONLY YOU	15
MY MORNING	16
HONEY	17
FORCES	18
MY SUPERHERO	19
CHAOS	20
CELEBRATION	21
SWEET SEPTEMBER	22
SURRENDERED	23
BEYOND THE SHADOWS	24
I TRUST YOU	25
SILVER LINING	26
WHEN I'M GONE	27
PLEASE FORGIVE ME	29
PROMISE ME	31
YOU AND I	32
CINDERGIRL	34
THE GARDEN	35
THE LAST VERSE	37
WHO ARE YOU I HAVE LOVED?	38
RIGHT OR WRONG	39
UNBRIDLED	41
IT'S NOT RIGHT	42
LOVE AND DUTY	43
MAGIC	45
CROSSROADS	46
ONE DAY	47
RETROSPECTION	48
2021	49
THE VESSEL	50
A HEAVY HEART	51
UNOWNED	52
THE MYSTERY OF WHITE ROSES	53
TO TRUST IN HIM	54
WILL TOMORROW COME?	55

YOUR TOMORROW	57
MOONLIGHT	58
A PARENTS' PRAYER	59
DEAR SON	61
I WILL REMEMBER YOU	63
INTO THE LIGHT	65
TO TRANQUIL SHORES	66
SPIDER'S WEB	67
THE ENDS OF EARTH	68
ASCENDING MOUNT OLYMPUS	70
EACH DAY	71
CHERISHED	72
IN THIS DARK CORNER OF THE UNIVERSE	74
TO SMILE	75
MOMENTOUS MOMENT	76
THE MAGIC WORDS	77
MY HOME	78
WE THANK THEE, LORD	79
FAITH AND REASON	80
MY POTTER, MY MAKER, MY LOVE	82
WHEN A FLAME DIES	83
REST IN FAITH	84
HE WILL NEVER BREAK YOUR HEART	86
SEARCH, SHINE, AND SHARE	88
MEET ME THERE	89
TO LIVE	91
THE ONE I LOVE	92
IF WE BUT CARE	93
THE TREE	95
THE PAUSE	97
I'LL STAY WITH YOU	99
DEATHBED	101
COMPLETION	102
TIMELESS	103
DISTANT PAST	104
BEHOLD	105
THE VOID	106
THE RIDES	107

THE LITTLE BIRD	108
CLOUDS	109
BUTTERFLY	110
OUR UNIVERSE	111
I MISS YOU	113
APART	114
MAKING LOVE	115
CONVICTION	117
DAMAGED	118
LETTING GO	119
END OF SEASON	120
COMMENCEMENT	121
SPLINTER	122
MEMORY	123
TESTS	124
INVISIBLE	125
POINT OF NO RETURN	126
AGED	127
GLORY OF LOVE	128
CHIRON	129
STRANGER	130
LA CORONA	131
THE NEW GARDEN	132
CULMINATION	133
NEVER-ENDING	134

OUR LOVE

Our love is...
The north star in the bleakest nights,
The rainbow past the strongest storm,
The cotton clouds upon the skies,
The dew that drenches the leaves at morn.

Our love is...
The voice of violins and lyres,
The song of larks and nightingales,
The baby's first laughter and smile,
The sweet symphony of angels.

Our love is...
The endless waves on the seashore,
The bedrock underneath the sea,
The essence of clean water,
The timelessness of eternity.

I WILL LOVE YOU

I will love you patiently,
Like a mother with her son,
I will love you tirelessly,
Like bees producing honey.

I will adore you in inspiring spring,
Savor in the summit of summer,
I will hold your hand in autumn,
And hug you tight in winter.

I will love you endlessly,
Like the waves of the ocean.
I will love you infinitely,
Like the stars in the heavens.

I will love you patiently and tirelessly,
In spring, summer, autumn and winter,
I will love you endlessly and infinitely,
Beyond lifetimes, beyond all possibilities.

ONLY YOU

In my bleak and barren world,
Only you have blossomed flowers,
And filled the air with songs.

In my deadlock circumstance,
Only you have opened alleys,
And paved paths to eminence.

Though my wings are broken,
Though my hands are tied,
Though my steps are numbered...

My mind muses, my heart longs,
My soul seeks for none other
Than my one and only you.

MY MORNING

To wake up in the morning
With you in my heart
Is the sweetest melody.

To see the sun rise
With you in my mind
Is like a dream come true.

To hear the birds sing
With you in my soul
Is my destiny.

Even now that us
Being together
May not yet be reality.

HONEY

You are to me
The sweetest melody,
The fragrance of flowers,
The flavor of honey...

A genuine gift of nature -
The honey that healed my wounds,
The honey that sealed my aches,
The honey that doesn't decay.

The honey that gives me strength
To wake up each day,
The honey that makes me smile
In its pure, unselfish way.

FORCES

When two celestial beings
Have cores composed of things
That fuel each other
And complete one another...

No matter the distance,
No matter the disturbance,
No matter the hindrance,
They will come in abeyance...

To what has been destined,
Though other celestial bodies intervene,
Each exerting its penultimate force
Not to let their union run its course...

Because this universe may not yet be ready
For their eventual, inevitable union,
Whose immense essence can form another galaxy
That will recreate the magic of creation.

MY SUPERHERO

Your heart is tender like Superman,
No less romantic than Captain America,
Not to say filthy rich like Batman,
And a brilliant strategist like Ironman.

You're moves are suave like Zorro,
A champion of the needy like Robin Hood,
You've saved me from a thousand sorrows,
You are and always will be my superhero.

CHAOS

Love, an asteroid landed on earth,
And the world has never been the same,
Beliefs were shaken, bonds were shattered,
Homes were abandoned, vows were broken....

Love, a force, impacted my life,
And every perception changed,
Boundaries dissolved, ensuing strife,
And long-accepted notions challenged.

What is true? What is real? What is right?
What is time? What is place? What is life?
I don't know anything anymore
Except that you're the one I truly love.

After all destructions and restructuring,
After all fleeting maxims dissolving,
Love needs to refine everything
To build on earth our heaven everlasting.

CELEBRATION

Each day, the dawn is sparkling,
The birds can't cease singing,
Even the sun is smiling,
For a morning greeting...

When two hearts,
Though far apart,
Can't seem to part,
No matter what...

No distance, no bondage,
No pain, no heartache,
No other force on earth,
Can tear apart or break...

The bond, the union,
The love, the communion,
The heavenly connection,
That deserves a celebration.

SWEET SEPTEMBER

One sweet September,
The gates of heaven opened,
And made bridges,
Where lovers can meet
Unencumbered.

When songs of love
Can reach their hearts,
And not law or man,
Or anything under the sun
Can hinder.

When there will never be
Heartache or longing,
Or fear or worry,
Because their intimacy
Outlasts anything.

They will always remember –
The day the heavens opened
A pathway to forever,
When love will never waiver,
One sweet September.

SURRENDERED

I had been humiliated and hurt,
Cursed like a whore,
Interrogated like a criminal,
Strangled like a stray animal.

I had been spied and spanked,
Blamed like a bitch,
Investigated and tried,
Hunted like a witch.

I had been silenced and stifled,
Treated like a fool,
Presumed, misjudged,
And labelled deranged.

I had been battered and bruised
Within and without,
But none hurt as much,
As giving up on us.

BEYOND THE SHADOWS

To see your face in the sunrise,
To hear you whisper in the rain,
To feel your touch in the moonbeams,
To long to meet you once again.

For every yearning of my heart
Brings us all the more apart,
For every longing of my soul
Grows between us a rising wall.

Let me not gaze at you in the day,
Let me not hold your hand and say –
I am just here beyond the shadows,
Only you to love and care.

I TRUST YOU

I trust your love
That has endured
Aeons of waiting.

I trust your love
That has shielded
Me from suffering.

I trust your love
That has showered
Surprising blessings.

I trust your love
Will endure, bless, and shield
Despite all space and longing.

SILVER LINING

My heart tonight is like the clouds –
Dark, heavy, and about to explode,
My heart that once was feather-light,
Passion-pink, and singing with delight.

My eyes tonight are like the clouds –
With torrents of outpouring rain,
My eyes that once were twinkling stars,
Now soaked in sorrow, fright and pain.

My soul tonight is like the clouds –
After the rain, gets lost and wanders,
My soul that once was sure had found
Its missing piece, and twin flame.

My heart, my eyes, my soul tonight
Are dimming and drowning in pain,
Yet though dark clouds may dim all light,
Tomorrow the sun might shine again.

WHEN I'M GONE

When I'm gone and you miss me,
Just close your eyes,
And listen to your heart,
For there I'll always be.

I'll warm you with the sunshine;
I'll smile on you with rainbows;
I'll hug you with the moonbeam;
I'll kiss you as the wind blows.

My spirit will always come to you
To greet you a great morning,
My soul will ease you through
The weariness in the evening.

My face will be carved on roses,
My tears in the falling rain,
My peace in the golden fishes,
My laughter in playing children.

I vow to never leave you
In joy and grief, in vigor and in pain,
My spirit will stay beside you
In light and gloom, in sun and rain.

PLEASE FORGIVE ME

Please forgive me
When I seem to hide
Traces of our history
Whenever threatened.

Please forgive me
If we cannot be
Always together,
To comfort and care.

Please forgive me
If I've been adamant
To my ideals despite
Despondency.

Please forgive me
If I willfully remain
True to my heart
In the face of adversity.

Please forgive me
If I hold on
To this devotion
Contrary to society.

PROMISE ME

Promise me –
You'll be well,
Strong and healthy,
Free from malady.

Promise me –
You'll be safe,
Secure and sound,
Free from enemy.

Promise me –
You'll be glad,
Joyful and blessed,
Free from misery.

Promise me -
You'll be well, safe, and glad,
Living your best life,
Happy and carefree.

YOU AND I

You and I are
Ice and fire,
Moon and Sun,
Reason and passion.

You and I are
North and south,
Lord and servant,
Heaven and earth.

You and I are
Black and white,
Night and day,
Left and right.

You and I are
Yang and yin,
Music and lyrics,
Water and sunlight.

You and I are
Not the same,
And though apart,
Are vital halves of one.

CINDERGIRL

At the moment of truth,
When the prince comes face-to-face
With the princess who captured his heart...

He finds out her golden carriage,
Footman, horses, coach, and ballgown,
Were momentary illusions...

That the woman he adored
Is not of royal blood nor noble origins,
Nor clad in splendor and glamor...

That the woman he loved
Has grimy feet and hands,
Tattered, subdued, wounded.

At the moment of truth,
Will the prince look into her eyes
The same way, and love her all over again?

THE GARDEN

Knowing you has been
A walk in the garden –
Breathtakingly beautiful,
But painfully fleeting.

Where flowers seem to bloom
Endlessly, and infinitely,
And hearts sing silent songs
That echo to eternity.

Where birds in cages can freely
Take care of each other devotedly,
And golden fishes can gather
Unencumbered together.

Where obstacles can be passed
Through beautiful bridges,
And rainbows seem to last
Amid spectacular sunsets.

Past pathways, and bridges,
Past flowers, and cages,
Past rainbows, and sunsets,
All strolls, like dreams, come to rest.

THE LAST VERSE

When the dream is over,
I wake up to reality –
That I am no creator,
Or mover, or leader,
But a mere property.

That expanding my mind,
Or honing my heart,
Or finding friends,
Is of less pertinence
Than serving my master.

Forgive me if I must
Keep the peace,
Turn off my light,
Stay silent
And follow.

WHO ARE YOU I HAVE LOVED?

Who are you I have loved?
You are the wind my wings can feel, yet cannot touch,
You are the sun with which I see, yet I cannot look.
In my heartbeat rings your voice I've never heard,
Which speaks only in my prayers as I ask God for you.
I've seen you in my dreams - a silhouette,
A nothingness that fills the emptiness in my heart,
That no handsome face or flirting tongue has ever quenched.
You I have resolved to wait in purity and innocence,
Even now without promises, avowals, or contracts.
You I have envisioned in every future moment -
In joy and pain, in calm and fuss, in life and death...
The only one I have ever loved, who are you?

RIGHT OR WRONG

What is sin?
What is not?
What is good?
What is bad?

What is wrong?
What is right?
What is truth?
What is lie?

If fulfilling my duty
Is what is right,
Then why is every cell in my body
Screaming to fight?

If loving somebody
Is morally wrong,
Then why are all cells in my body
Singing a song?

What is the greatest guide
To doing what is right?
Is it the law?
Or is it love?

UNBRIDLED

He was a wild horse with a strong spirit,
They bridled him to "keep him safe,"
The more he broke free, the tighter it got...

I tried to tame him in patience and compassion,
Attune to his emotions, let his spirit roam,
But they wouldn't let me....

Alas, in a relentless battle of wills,
His spirit had triumphed to break free
From the empty shell of his choked, bridled body.

They both won –
They had his body,
And he had his spirit.

IT'S NOT RIGHT

It's not right
To think of you night and day
To dream of your smile
To peer into your eyes
And feel your soul.

It's not right
To wish you joy and happiness
To make you smile
To put sparkle in your eyes
And fire to your soul.

It's not right
To accept your love and protection
To always make my heart smile
To dry the tears from my eyes
And free my enslaved soul.

LOVE AND DUTY

There was once a lady
Who wed out of duty,
Her life has been normal,
Nothing magical,
Nothing tragical.

She found passion
In her profession,
Her life has been exceptional,
Her work historical,
Her roles singular.

Until true love came,
And nothing's been the same,
Her life has become magical,
Her days extra-special,
Her moments spectacular.

Until duty demanded
What society dictated,
Her life has become tragical,
Her moments drab and dull,

Imprisoned in a sacred vow.

Can true love set her free?
Perhaps it has already,
Her heart is not anymore confined,
Nor her spirit imprisoned,
She has learned...

To hope,
To endure,
To persevere,
Against all odds,
Beyond distance and time.

MAGIC

I used to think that magic
Comes like a clash of lightning
Paraded with claps of thunder,
Or an imposing high-noon sun
That commands surrender.

So when heaven decided to pour
Your love like a gentle rain,
I was lost in search for storms,
For a distant throbbing heart
Helplessly conquered...

Only to find the magic of your love,
Like the whispered song of the rainbow,
Or the silent beams of the dawn.
Only to learn that the truest passion
Nurtures like the dew of the morn.

Love is not war, but peace,
Nor is it insanity or loss of mind.
It may begin as a seed, and grow
However slowly and painfully,
To a strong, giant, dependable oak.

CROSSROADS

I now stand before this vastness,
Not knowing where to go,
Like every turn is a dead-end maze,
Yet to stand still is to stop time,
Is to stop the heartbeat,
And to go back is defeat.

Must I choose between loving,
And being loved?
When loving means facing
Shooting arrows that pierce the heart,
Yet being loved means ice castles,
That will imprison my passions.

ONE DAY

One day we'll walk
Barefooted and tear-stained
Past thornbushes and shadowlands...

Knowing that beyond the dark clouds
And smashing rains, there's a place of healing
Where rainbows never end.

Like an indelible insignia in the skies,
As in our hearts - a promise of love,
Of life, of homecoming and deliverance.

This day, the promised land seems
Just a dream, one day, these shadowlands
Will only seem a nightmare.

RETROSPECTION

Sometime in my journey I will look back,
And ponder on the path I've trodden...
Perhaps I will just laugh over my tears,
And pat my shoulders for licking my own wounds,
While climbing cold mountains in thin air.

Yet surely my heart will swell with pride,
That the only punctuation of my weeks
Has been the assembly of the elect -
Thriving in zealous songs and genuine worship,
Abounding in steadfast faith and enduring love.

Should I ask my years where they have gone,
They will answer, "We have gone to your God,
To whom you have sent us..."
Only then can I look ahead,
To step the last steps of my sojourn.

2021

A year of love and loss,
Of despair and repair,
Of ending and starting anew.

It must have been
The retreat of winter and fall
To pave the way for spring.

It has been tough,
It has been sweet,
And then, tranquil.

It has been tiring,
It has been testing,
But never surrendered.

It is a year worth noting –
As alive, vibrant and silent,
As the music of the heartbeat.

THE VESSEL

It was a rather simple vessel
In the keeping of a Healer.
It contained a potent potion
That stirred nerves, and enflamed
Still hearts from near-death.

The vessel became renowned,
Was abducted by treachers,
And employed in wicked wiles.
Its potion became a poison
To everyone's disdain.

The vessel longed for the Healer
And realized its worthlessness –
It was the same vessel,
With the same spirit,
Only in the hands of a different master.

A HEAVY HEART

The stage shook with a round of applause,
Drowned in a blinding spotlight
That never seemed to cease...

Alighting from the stairs,
There was a flood of smiles,
Trembling of knees, shaking of hands.

Amid the grandeur and glory,
Was the heaviest of hearts,
That pondered on its gravity.

Why was not the heart delighted?
What stirred from within? No one
Knew, not even the heart-bearer.

UNOWNED

Perhaps all the angels
Know your name,
I've so passionately
Whispered
In my most
Solemn prayers.

'Tis enough for me
That you are safe,
Cared for,
Loved,
Enveloped in someone's
Warmth and kisses.

THE MYSTERY OF WHITE ROSES

There is a certain charm in the white rose,
Something not just fair and pure,
But crystal-clear and mystical,
That will always capture my imaginings.

Indeed, this moment has blessed me,
A stroll on a path sprinkled with white roses,
How elegant they look, dancing with their verdant escorts,
As the wind plays a silenced waltz,
In a bedroom curtained with lavender.

But I do not want to see them merely,
So my weak fingers fell on one costumed body,
Only to unfold the mystery -
Of a white rose stained red,
Quite reluctant to dance with the heavy downpour
As curtains close.

TO TRUST IN HIM

Oftentimes, I'm lost
And entangled in a web
Of disarray and confusion...

And I just want to flee
To an arid land to dry
The tears that well inside...

But my heart's too heavy,
And my wings too tired
To flap away from fright...

So I stay, and pray.
All at once the rays of day
Come shining bright...

To clear my sight of tears,
And melt away my fears,
Because this web I'm entangled with...

Too soon to be revealed,
Is but a dazzling robe spun
To shame my strength, to trust in Him.

WILL TOMORROW COME?

In crushing pain she rallies hope,
Inside her brain, the tumor grows,
The beauty once to her bestowed
Is now impaired by drunken gait,
Half-rigid face and vision hazed.

The life she carries in her womb
Has bloomed, but horror looms.
That each moment, each heartbeat,
Each breath may be their last –
"Will tomorrow come?" they ask.

With all the courage she can muster,
She prepared her three other toddlers
Of her impending departure,
Yet in her heart she prays,
For them, a few more years to stay.

In all her agonies, she realizes,
That there is a God who listens,
There is a God who heals,
A God who wipes away all tears –

A God of infinite tomorrows.

She now sits, and smiles,
At her three toddlers and a newborn,
After surviving her brain operation.
She's twice as beautiful now,
Radiating life, hope, and faith.

YOUR TOMORROW

I hope all your tomorrows
Will be filled with
Sunshine and rainbows.

I hope all your tomorrows
Will be scattered with
Flowers and friends.

I hope all your tomorrows
Will be situated
Rock-solid and invincible.

I hope all your tomorrows
Will resound
With love and laughter.

If for peace and goodness' sake,
I may not be there,
Today, I'll celebrate your tomorrows.

MOONLIGHT

Tonight, my love,
I bask under the full moonlight;
No less mesmerized,
Than when I see your face.

Like the phases of the moon,
In all its beguiling beauty;
No less breathtaking,
Than our love story.

Sometimes it hides,
Sometimes it smiles,
No less enchanting,
Than when it glorifies.

Tonight, my love,
I'll savor the full moonlight;
Before our gleam comes quiet
In broad daylight.

A PARENTS' PRAYER

To You, O God, we offer
Out firstborn - the wonder of life
That You have blessed and entrusted
Us parents to perpetuate
In the continuum of eternity.

Kindly guide her in the labyrinth
Of human passions and aspirations,
That she may not go astray
From the perfect plan.
You have ordained her
Even before she was conceived.

Please mold her hands in diligence,
Her heart be forged in quiet strength,
Purity, humility, and servitude,
In her mind, imprinted your laws,
Which are the foundation of wisdom.

Alas, O God, please be her fortress
And her sanctuary in a world
Undergoing putrefaction,
That she may be a fragrant scent before You,
All the days of her dedicated life.

DEAR SON

As I look into your sparkling eyes,
I cannot help but be mesmerized,
How much great potential lies dormant
In that little eager flame in your soul -
I see you holding earth in the palm of your hand,
I see you kindling the world with your words,
I see you bridging timelines, opening wormholes,
I see you discerning universal laws yet unknown.

I treasure this moment, Son, with your little hand
Holding mine, and fondly reminisce -
How that little forearm blocked a blow meant for mom,
And punched a brute beast twice your meager frame,
How that little arm encircled my shivering shoulder,
Unnerved my sinews, unthawed my heart,
How those little lips delivered a thousand kisses,
To melt away my weariness and break my defenses.

I wish you to come home each day fulfilled,
With a welcoming smile as sparkling as you had,
With warm arms and kisses eagerly enveloping you,
With sons and daughters of your own raising to do

What you've always done, and after all the laughter,
You all succumb to the night in peaceful slumber.
I hope someday someone will continue to kiss you good night
For the rest of your sweet, serene, spectacular life.

I WILL REMEMBER YOU

I will remember You -
In the dawn of my life, as You nurture
Me with knowledge and strength to my peak,
As You direct my path away from
Pointless pursuits of human arrogance.

I will remember You -
In the depths of despair and solitude,
After fleeting moments of achievement,
In the heights of wisdom and discernment,
When pain has healed and toils have ended.

I will remember You -
As I march down the aisle to utter my vows,
In a union that will relive the magic of creation.
I will offer You the first fruits of my vineyard,
And leave unto You the choicest of my crops.

I will remember You -
Until You are the only one I can remember,
When even my memory of space and time has faded,
Till the shadow of death steals the last of my breath,
Till I am remembered no more...
I will remember You, My Lord.

INTO THE LIGHT

Oh weary soul
In anguish,
Groping and longing
For a ray of light,
Blindfolded by sin,
Betrayed to the scaffold
Of those sentenced
To death.

Heed our call,
Lost sheep of the fold!
Our hands reach out
As we were reached for before.
Open your eyes
Into the light
Where God awaits
To grant you life.

TO TRANQUIL SHORES

In the midst of an ocean of despair,
I know not where to go.
If I fight, the waves will pull me
Down to turbulent depths.
Even if I flap my arms with all my might,
All my might will be drained, futile,
And yet I am trapped in an enormity
That is far beyond me,
Beyond my wisdom, beyond my strength,
But not my faith.

So I close my eyes and rest my head
Against angry waters,
Though roaring waves bite into my flesh,
I close my eyes even tighter,
And rest further in the ocean of despair,
Knowing I have a Master,
Who alone is beyond all this enormity,
Who'll carry me to calmer currents,
Beyond depths, beyond turbulence,
To tranquil shores.

SPIDER'S WEB

The great spinner
Steps aback, like a god
Of the seventh day,
Muses at his ivory tower,
Silently patting himself
For a web well done,
While secretly pursuing
A prey for feast.

'Tis almost a triumphant
Jubilation, for sweetest are
The fruits of one's labor, but not
For rushing footfalls.
Another spinner's off to work,
Different species, different form,
Same fragile web,
Same fate.

THE ENDS OF EARTH

It is twilight,
Only a few more seconds left
Before a glint of light
Scatters this dense darkness.

Still, terror inhabits the Earth,
She wails with lava from her mouth.
Her seas stir, her grounds shake,
Her blood is noxious, she gasps for breath.

The man she cradles in her bosom
Is likewise desperate,
He's plagued with maladies unknown.
In hunger, he deteriorates.

He builds nation-states hoping to unite,
Only to further divide,
Into lands and ideologies for which he'll fight
To the expense of his brother's life.

He's still savoring the bitter fruit,
That from his previous paradise seclude,

By forming demi worlds of random blasts,
Thinking machines, evolving apes, and helpless gods.

In all this subjective greatness and wisdom,
Man has decided to terminate his own,
Exist like brute beast, and drown
In brief moments of hallucination.

The Earth, she wails; and Man, he screams;
Both are indeed suffering,
Yet the heart that can cure them
Is cold and wanting.

It is near daybreak,
But the greatest terror is yet to come,
When all those given the power to judge
Will be judged in accordance.

When all who chose the path that's right,
Will be chosen to tread the light,
And all who endured until the end
Will inherit a promised land.

ASCENDING MOUNT OLYMPUS

I am here tilling the foot
Of Mount Olympus, near
Shady trees and riverbanks,
Near lovebirds still
Getting to know each other.

I am here watching the multitude
Of men striving to be gods, creeping
Over steep and slippery slopes,
Over each other's backs, like crabs
In a spinster's basket.

I am here because nothing's
Up there, only eternal choking emptiness
Of bleak and barren mountains graphed
Against history books, yet to descend
Is to pass away as quietly as...

I am here.

EACH DAY

Each day is like a gift –
We have to unwrap,
Piece by piece,
Layer by layer,
In every second.

Each day is like a page –
We ought to write,
As fate provides,
Scene by scene,
The story of our lives.

Each day is a present –
We need to give,
To state our essence,
To serve the purpose
Of our earth-existence.

CHERISHED

"You are precious in my sight, and
Honored, and I love you."
You used to tell me I am cherished
As the apple of your eyes,
Even the strands of my hair are counted.

So I walked through life unencumbered by fears,
Like all flames in the universe are the same
As the warm hearth at home.
Not knowing deceit, I believed everything,
And everything, I believed, is good.

Till a scorching heat melted me like
Wax kneeling before a deaf tyrant.
Stabbing pain, so that was how it felt.
For a while,
I thought, "You are God, and I am man
What am I that you will be mindful of me?"

I never thought that when my soul was set afire,
I was kindled in Your arms,
Like a baby being bathed by its mother,

So that should I melt like wax,
I will be molded according to Your image.

Perhaps a century wiser and stronger,
All the more I believe that even
The strands of my hair are counted.
All the more I ask, " You are God, I am man,
What am I that You are mindful of me?"

IN THIS DARK CORNER OF THE UNIVERSE

In this dark corner of the universe,
I draft my castles,
And sing to my heart's desire.
When nobody, not even I,
Can bear my aches,
And all men are too sore
To be pained a little more,
Then this dark corner,
And this sweet silence,
And just a little faith,
Will make a castle and a song,
To heal the afflictions
In my soul.

TO SMILE

Smile. Laugh. Hope. Love.
Climb. Run. Fly!

Hold. Trust. Hope. Touch.
Blink. Break. Sigh.

Ask. Walk? Hide. Walk?
Stand. Walk? Try.

Love. Cry. Hope. Cry.
Rest. Pray. Smile!

MOMENTOUS MOMENT

Close your eyes to see your soul,
Stay silent and let your heart speak,
Listen to a song you've never heard before,
As you succumb to the power of His spirit.

Experience eternity in a moment,
Savor this parcel of paradise,
Let Him be your only armament,
Let Him clear the mist from your eyes.

He's been waiting for you, cherished creation,
Ever since the world needed water and light,
Come back to Him and rebuild the union,
Praise Him with all your soul, heart, and might.

Let not this memory leave your cognition,
You have experienced the greatest wisdom,
You have fulfilled the sole duty of man.
Open your eyes, arise, and face the world again.

THE MAGIC WORDS

Long before the Tower of Babel had fallen,
Man had continued to patch the broken
Language that might pave the path to heaven,
And yet, the magic words remained unspoken
Because knowledge had filled the hearts of men...

To the point of folly. Poor creatures, fallen
Angels, whose wings and hopes were broken,
Desperately longing for a piece of heaven.
If only they can hear the unspoken
Words deeply embedded in the hearts of men.

Long before the Garden of Eden had fallen
For wisdom, when the first law was broken.
Still, the path back to heaven
Had been purposely laid on words better unspoken-
The magic mantra that will merge the hearts of men.

MY HOME

I love your house, my Lord,
It has been my home.
In the silence of its home are shimmering chimes,
In its tranquility there is festivity of souls and angels,
In its confines there is freedom from guilt and pain,
In its apparent vulnerability there is strength and security,
In the simplicity of its truth lies the deepest wisdom,
In here I close my eyes and see the brightest light I've known,
I would want to live in that light, my Lord,
And stay here with You in Your house forever.

WE THANK THEE, LORD

We thank Thee, Lord with all our might
That though the world's descending plight
Looms on mankind like the night,
You sent Your stars to be our light,
You sent Your guides to show the right
Less-traveled path to everlasting life.

We thank Thee, Lord with all our hearts,
We praise Thy name with all our souls,
You gather us to be one flock,
From ends of earth, You brought us home.
You washed our sins to dazzling white,
You blessed our lives, You called Your own.

FAITH AND REASON

I used to climb our roof,
Watch a falling star,
Wish, and doze off happily,
Till I was asked to prove,
If God exists, then where is He?

I searched my heart, the heights, the depths,
Where mysteries too ordered to be chance,
And life, too vast and perfect to evolve,
Clearly point to an awesome Creator,
Who's simply everywhere.

Still, men are so wise in their eyes,
Believing only what is seen, and
Beyond reasonable doubt, proven
By their own fragile minds whose power
So easily flickers.

Whereas others, for too much faith,
Neglected reason, now fooled and slaved,
Yet still holding on, tight and adamant
To doctrines that mock their logic

Face to face.

Now freed from reason and deception,
Blessed with faith in truth,
I still climb our roof,
Watch for falling stars,
Pray and doze off peacefully.

MY POTTER, MY MAKER, MY LOVE

Your bare hands formed me from dust,
Warmed with a breath of life and consciousness,
To know You, the Potter who has been molding me
Into something and someone.

Once lost in a world where flickering wisdom
Guides a labyrinth of wealth and power,
You lifted me into the rising sun you've chosen,
You made me a shining ray of truth.

I was dust, my days were numbered,
And You snatched me from death,
To nurture, to kindle, to love,
To be Your own dear one.

My Potter, My Maker, My Love,
I offer You my strength, my soul, myself,
However humble I, in serving You,
Shall transcend the bounds of life.

WHEN A FLAME DIES

The cold December wind
Steals the last flame of my lamp.
Blindly, I scribbled, borrowing
Radiance from a reluctant half-moon,
When once crescent, cradled
Lovers in its arms,
Smiling sweetly on Summer's eve.

Smiling sweetly amid the cold December wind,
Reminiscing how it felt to be cradled
In your arms, when our flame
Could only shame the fiery stars,
Till the cold December wind
Steals the last spark of your love,
Blindly, I traced the scars
Your embers etched
In my burnt and chilling heart.

REST IN FAITH

Rest, dear heart, rest in the bed of innocence.
Let not a whisper, or a song,
Or wisdom and compatibility,
Or an angelic face and its bouquet of promises
Awake you from your peaceful slumber.

Hush now, dear heart, the world is noisy indeed,
Perhaps it is just too eager to crush thy shell,
To see what gem lies inside. But do not be disturbed,
Gold must stand the test of fire,
And diamonds remain unscathed.

Be still, dear heart, be pure, be untouched,
Do not be afraid, for the mountains are too great a guard.
Neither should you hate time, she is your servant,
Like the tides of the sea, she gently sweeps away
The footprints of them who try to invade.

Sleep in peace, dear heart, and sooner than you expect,
Your Father shall bless you with someone
Whose arms have long awaited your warmth.
He shall be your guard, your army, and your castle,
Your strength for the rest of your blissful, awakened
Moments; but for now, dear heart, rest in faith.

HE WILL NEVER BREAK YOUR HEART

If you're looking for a true love,
That's ever fresh and new,
Then search no more just look above,
The Lord has longed for you.

If you're pained and hurt so badly,
For love that's torn apart,
Then turn to God, He'll never leave you,
He will never break your heart.

If you miss Him, He's not absent
Beyond the starry skies,
Though His love may seem divided,
The more it multiplies.

Love the Lord with your whole being,
Offer Him your life,
Through thick and thin just trust in Him,
He will never break your heart.

Then at the right time, He will find

Who you've been searching for,
In joy and peace, not two but one,
You'll love Him all the more.

Though too soon your life may end,
God's love will never part from
Your children and grandchildren,
He will never break your heart.

SEARCH, SHINE, AND SHARE

Search for truth, search for wisdom, search for love,
To top it all, search the will of God,
Never rest assured,
Till they're yours for good,
They're the greatest treasures you can ever have.

Once you have truth, faith, and love in your heart,
Let them lead your way and light your path,
Even when suppressed,
Even when repressed,
Hold on to them and never let them part.

Then your glow can never be hidden,
Leading others to trod the path you've taken,
In sharing your light,
It multiplies,
You'll shine like the brightness of the heavens.

MEET ME THERE

Far from the madding crowd,
Where their shouts and curses become distant,
Muted, and transformed to soothing love songs.

Where shackles are broken
And prisoners freed, where sentences
And contracts are unsealed, like birds uncaged.

Let us fly to that secret place
Where roses bloom, stars shine,
And the scent of lavender fills the air.

Where terror and fright
May be melted while enwrapped
In warm hands, hot hugs, and passionate kisses.

Where doubt and confusion
May be cleared with liberation,
That only the blending of twin souls know of.

Where love cannot be silenced,
Where every second is forever,
But forever is too short.

Where there is no space or time,
Only unfathomable bliss, rainbows, and union
Of long departed halves, meet me there.

TO LIVE

Can anyone teach us what it is to live?
Is it to exist from day to day?
To feed, to sleep, to breathe?

Can anyone instruct us where to live?
Is it the earth, the wind, the sky?
Or is it the towers, the palace, the stars?

Can anyone guide us when to live?
Is it the brash, dazzling, blooming seedling?
Or is it the mellow, seasoned, adjourning sage?

Can anyone enlighten us why to live?
Is it the blossom in the bosom and the womb?
Or is it the mission, the vision and the commission?

Can anyone show us how to live?
Is it to choose, to dream, to do?
Or to laugh, to love, to relish?

Can anyone really grasp
What, where, when, why, and how to live?
Or is it all of all, and simple? To live.

THE ONE I LOVE

The one I love
Is a tower,
In stance
And status.

The one I love
Is the air,
Always there
To comfort and care.

The one I love
Is an eagle,
Steadily flying high
Amidst any storm.

The one I love
Is my tower, my air, my eagle,
My fierce protector,
My source of life and adventure.

IF WE BUT CARE

If we but care to see
The breathtaking tapestry
Of soft, iridescent hues
Cast in the skies at dawn...

If we but care to listen
Long before we awaken
To the sweet serenade of birds
Greeting us a beautiful morn...

If we but care to feel
The cool breeze like a soft kiss,
The warm embrace of sunrise,
The caress of gently flowing water...

If we but care to notice
The countless gifts
Endlessly showered upon us
Day after day after day...

Then we will realize
How special we are,
How valued in the eyes
Of a doting, loving Creator.

THE TREE

Propped like a statesman,
Beaming with elegance -
If it's not beauty that depicts the tree,
What else could it be?

In its sturdy trunk
Is inscribed a history,
A timeline can be found
In the heart of the tree.

The patterns of its branches
Display astounding intricacy,
The richness of its foliage
Shames a woman's crowning glory.

Like stars in the night sky
Are its florets in full bloom,
It springs the fountain of life
From its breath and its womb.

In its silence is a strength
That withstands the test of time,
In its beauty, wisdom, and worth,
What can even be more sublime?

THE PAUSE

What makes music?
Is it just the notes,
The highs and lows,
Or the silence in between?

What makes a container?
Is it just the perimeter,
That surrounding structure,
Or the empty space within?

What makes the universe?
Is it just the stars,
Planets and galaxies,
Or the vast expanse suspending?

What makes time?
Is it just the seconds,
Hours, days, and months,
Or the interval mediating?

What makes life?
Is it always movement,
Happening, reaching, achieving,
Or the silent moments pursuing nothing?

I'LL STAY WITH YOU

I'll stay with you
Through the rain,
To dry your pain,
To be your rainbow.

I'll stay with you
When you're confused,
When lights diffuse,
I'll boost your focus.

I'll stay with you
When you're in doubt,
When fears paralyze,
I'll be your antidote.

I'll stay with you
At the height of fever,
Whenever you shiver,
My arms will cover.

When you feel blue,
When all are lost and gone,
When you're back to none,
I'll stay with you.

DEATHBED

After a long weary day
In your elegant glass-walled office,
Untangling the mess of human relations,
Maintaining fiscal health of corporations,
You arrive late at night,
In your hard-earned mansion,
To lay down your worn-out head
In your king size bed,
As the endless chatter of your colleagues
Still haunts your dreams.

Work is life, and life, work,
As days turn to decades swiftly,
Snatching the vitality of the body,
And no matter how much you've earned,
Or what unfathomable wisdom you've learned,
One day, you have to face the end,
To rest your worn-out head once again.
Of all the accomplishments and belongings
You've spent your whole life earning,
In your deathbed, what can you bring?

COMPLETION

The right and left brain
Are not at all the same,
Not even mirrors in function.

Each of the right and left eyes
Cover a portion of vision
Blind to the other.

The body and the soul,
Though divergent in form
Must converge to be human.

For a man is a woman,
Distinctly from another dimension,
Yet uniquely his completion.

TIMELESS

The concept of time has been
As old as time itself,
And it has been too handy
An abstraction.

What if there is really
No past or future?
Only an endless
Present.

Is it really possible
That what we do today
May undo a past,
And rewrite history?

The greatest rebellion
In the history of man
Will be the abolition
Of time.

DISTANT PAST

Why am I always looking
At recent events like
They were a distant past?

As if submerged in an ocean,
All voices are muffled,
And all sights dimmed.

Why is there no clinging
To the valued memories
I've been delicately compiling?

Like there's no past, present,
Or future, all collapsing
To what can now be felt and seen.

BEHOLD

Behold, the Almighty Lord,
From His heavenly abode –
When we deem alone,
He sees our deeds,
And hears our pleas.

Behold, the Lord of Hosts,
Who rallies His army -
When we thought we've lost,
He fights our battles silently,
And wins our wars discreetly.

Behold, the King of Kings,
The owner of everything -
When we seem to have nothing,
He opens gates, rivers, and endings,
To grant us unexpected blessings.

THE VOID

Matter is anything
That occupies
Space, and to others,
All that matters.

Yet in space,
There are places
Where matter
Does not matter.

In search for things,
A significant finding
Is sometimes missing,
And that is nothing.

The void, the vacuum,
The matterless space,
The beginning, the ending,
Of all possibilities.

THE RIDES

Life is one beautiful adventure
Of exciting rides and trips
To the once unknown.

To unchartered seas and valleys,
Mountains and oceans,
Creatures and cultures.

To a roller-coaster of emotions,
Peak of exhilarating heights,
And trough of loosening lows.

Emerging from the once feared
By knowing and experiencing,
Riding, feeling, and passing.

THE LITTLE BIRD

Up above the walls,
The little bird flies
Among branches.

Singing merrily
In a dawn chorus
Among other little birds.

Relishing the moment,
Oblivious of any requirement
For nourishment.

I am you, little bird,
Unknown yet uncaged,
Content with its gift of song.

CLOUDS

Mama, when rain pours,
Do clouds cry?
While they don't have wings,
How can they fly?

Mama, how do clouds taste?
Are they sweet?
Are they real cotton candies,
Like gifts that drift?

Mama, are there really castles
Above the clouds?
Can you bring me up there,
When I'm scared of crowds?

BUTTERFLY

Who knows the journey
You've travelled painfully,
From an icky caterpillar
Devouring leaves and flowers.

Who knows the solitude
You've endured with fortitude,
Enveloped in your cocoon,
Not knowing when you'll be reborn.

Now beautiful, majestic butterfly,
Who steals a glance as you pass by,
Standing tall, flying free and high,
Surpassing life's mandatory trials.

OUR UNIVERSE

There is a universe
Where you and I
Walk hand in hand
Carefree and unhindered...

Beside the seashore,
With the waves of the sea
Kissing our soles
And calming our souls.

In a serene garden,
With blooming flowers
Carpeting our paths
And warming our hearts.

Around our own sweet home,
With the laughter of our daughters
Filling the walls and halls,
Like music to our ears.

Till the last of our days,
With our loving memories,
Like the sunset of our lives,
Still shining in our minds.

I MISS YOU

I miss you
Like how the lock
Misses its key,
Every time it's closed.

I miss you
Like how the yin
Misses its yang,
In the circle of life.

I miss you
Like how the dove
Misses the wind,
While it's flying.

I miss you
Like how the body
Misses its soul,
The essence of its being.

APART

Sometimes, people and things
Who are meant to be together
Are designed to be apart.

Like the legs of a table,
Or the limbs of a chair,
Like the pillars of Parthenon.

Any closer will crumble
The whole structure,
Stronger when farther.

They have to be apart
To be a vital part
Of a greater purpose.

MAKING LOVE

What greater magic is there
Than the merging of two souls?
When even their heartbeats
Pound in symphony,
To an ardent dance
That can rock the foundations
Of sobriety and society.

What greater beauty is portrayed
In the union of opposites,
In the juxtaposition
Of light and dark,
Of weak and strong,
Of yin and yang,
Of lines and songs.

What greater blessing is reached
At the pinnacle of delight,
Once a powerful blast
Has been unleashed,
And serenity reigns,
Enveloping the united
In the warm flame of love
Whence it all began, and never ends.

CONVICTION

Each night upon the stars I whisper plea,
As I trace your face among speckled void,
That you, My Love, be here to dine with me,
The once unsavored feast be most enjoyed;
Reveling in your kisses more than wine,
Elated with the lightness of your touch,
And in your gaze, how constellations shine!
No other sight on earth delights me much.
But we, My Love, are prisoners of fate,
Chastened to a lifetime yoke and barrier,
With sky-high walls impervious to love's spate,
What's sealed and joined can't be put asunder.
Thus every night the stars will hear my cry
For I will never yield our love to die.

DAMAGED

You cautioned me –
That you're damaged,
Scarred and scared.

I was well pleased –
If you had been whole,
There'd be no more space.

I forewarn you too -
I, too, am damaged,
Flawed and afraid.

It's just so wonderful –
How our jagged edges jive
To form a heart that's whole.

LETTING GO

I love you
With a love
That never owns.

Your smile
Will be my smile,
However it may hurt.

Your decision
Is my legislation,
Final and irrevocable.

I love you so
To let you go
Where your heart longs.

Once your wings
Are weary,
I vow, in me
You'll always have a home.

END OF SEASON

When you were orphaned,
I held you in my arms,
Because you needed a mother,
And discreetly paved your path,
To carry on the counsel of your father.

I saw you grow in strength and power,
Won wars, conquered kingdoms,
Now, elegant on your throne,
My time has come,
My task is done.

No matter how beautiful the petals
Of a dear and charming flower,
When it's time to fructify, they fall.
Even the sun spectacularly sets,
To reveal a glimpse of the universe.

My dearest, my beloved,
It may be time to unhold a hand,
And succumb to the celestial plan,
In a carefully calculated world,
All events have been designed.

COMMENCEMENT

As we march down the aisle,
Your little hand holding mine,
Seems like we're passing through
A point of no return.

No matter how cute and funny
Our olden and golden days were,
Destiny is often uncanny
To transform us upwardly.

In the span of time given
To every human being,
Each chapter is a challenge,
Every ending a beginning.

As you step to each next level
Of greater responsibility and power,
My promise is your hand in mine,
We'll transcend all trials together.

SPLINTER

There is a splinter
Stabbed in my heart,
It will be a fatal error
To pull it apart.

There is a splinter
Stuck in my eye,
Tears flow like a river,
Can't bid it goodbye.

Why are rules drafted to tie
And imprison two persons for life,
For a choice once deemed right
By their unenlightened mind?

Why can't two souls be set free
From a bondage laid by society,
When outside the confines of their prison
The universe awaits their expansion?

MEMORY

Life is a collection
Of action-pictures stored
In the mind.

But when the packets
Of memory-containing cells
Are filled, what's left?

Where can moments
Be reminisced? Where can
Loved ones be found?

Baffling, but at times
The heart is too familiar
To matters dimmed in mind.

TESTS

Our love has undergone scrutiny,
To prove its sterling quality,
For something far more worthy
Than gold, diamond, or any jewelry,
Confirms its authenticity,
However unintentionally,
All the more persistently.

Is it true gold? To appraise,
Will acid make it waste?
To evaluate if it's true love,
Can it survive whatever hurt?
Like diamond, is it pure and stark?
Only if in the depths of its heart
No other love can leave a mark.

Will our love abide
The test of time?
Will it not slowly die,
Yet be more sublime,
Will it bloom after a storm,
Even in drought, be strong?
So far, our love surpassed it all.

INVISIBLE

In a cosmos where images
Form the foundation
Of people's persona,

In a cutthroat society
Where faces are obliged
To stick out to be seen,

I choose to be invisible,
And contribute incognito,
From a serene secret space,

Not knowing my disgrace,
Disability, and deprivation,
Has become my superpower.

POINT OF NO RETURN

There will come a moment
When we've travelled so far
That there's no turning back.

Though the memory of home
Is enticing, we've become
A wanderer welcomed.

For some, the stretching
Reaches a point of parting
That warrants no returning.

For a fortunate few,
In tribulations are found
An inseparable bond.

AGED

Many people fear wrinkles,
Age spots, frail bones,
Poor hearing and weak eyesight...

But with you by my side,
Holding my feeble hand,
And kissing my wrinkled brow...

When we don't even need
Words to understand
What our hearts loudly speak...

When we don't even have
To look at each other's eyes
To see our merged souls...

And when our kisses taste even
Better than an aged wine,
Our aging I fear not, but dearly yearn.

GLORY OF LOVE

In a rather harsh world,
Where the tenderest emotions
Are crushed or subdued...

Where the prevailing concern
Day after day is sheer
Survival and preservation...

Where rigid societal norms
Create detention of souls,
Long longing for liberation...

The angels are keenly watching.
If a love that barely bloomed
In the hardest circumstance...

Can sustain its ardent magic,
Fervently endure all sufferings,
And emerge in stunning glory.

CHIRON

He touches them, the feeble and weak;
He looks at their anguish, and feels their ache;
He pours his heart and soul and intellect,
And restores the vigor to them, once sick.

Notwithstanding the peril he faces,
In every contagion he boldly encounters,
In sleeplessness, exhaustion, and sacrifice,
His faithfulness radiates to each life he touches.

The lives revived are his greatest treasures,
Not wages, riches, or being famous,
Yet no one knows the disease he endures,
The wounded healer may never recoup.

STRANGER

Strange, but sometimes,
We fall for someone
We thought we knew...

Still, the ebb of time
Reveals an entirely
Different entity.

Stranger, when someone
Recognizes another,
Just encountered...

Like they've known each other
For several lifetimes,
Inseparable in any circumstance.

LA CORONA

It's a simple RNA wrapped in protein,
An exquisite work of art, like a crown,
That claimed millions of human lives.

Suddenly, the streets are almost empty,
The air is clear, the poor are fed,
The seats of wealth and power filled with dread.

What the socialists strived for centuries,
La corona did in weeks -
A free flow of wealth and equity for air.

Locked in their own homes,
Families once fragmented are united,
And people have time and passion to pray.

Like letters, words, encryptions,
All DNAs and RNAs are codes –
La Corona may be a message...

From Life itself to Man,
When we have learned to deeply understand,
She'll cease her work and return home.

THE NEW GARDEN

Where magic begins
At the end of a rainbow,
The new garden blooms.

The giant peacock
Welcomes a Lilliputian
On top of jade stairs.

Cascading flowers
And two huge butterflies guard
A hidden chess match.

The colossal bear
Offers its comforting hug
Past a trail of hearts.

Drowning in sweetness,
The candies of Candyland
Echo affections.

A piece of heaven
Gifted to afflicted earth;
Beauty is healing.

CULMINATION

It seems eons ago when He started
Tilling the soil and planting seeds,
Day by day in loving patience,
He watered His plants and pulled out the weeds.
Not counting the days His plants fructified
And showered Him blessings in abundance.

It seems eons ago when He started
Tilling the mind and planting knowledge,
Day by day in arduous perseverance,
He did His homework, complied requirements.
Too occupied to notice the nearing fruition,
He's marching to herald His glorious graduation.

It seems eons ago when he started
Tilling her heart and planting love songs,
Day by day in caring forbearance,
He nurtured passion in her fragile emotions.
Months passed like days, weeks mere seconds,
Till holding his hand, she vowed her devotion.

NEVER-ENDING

In the beginning
Was the look,
And the look was with love,
And the look was love...

And then, a smile,
A word, a handshake,
A message, a conversation,
A connection, a relation...

A union stretched apart,
Obstacles, hindrances,
Prohibitions, persecution,
Prolonged separation...

Bridges, networks,
Butterflies, rainbows,
Lifetimes, but one love
Endures and never ends.